4x4
Vehicles

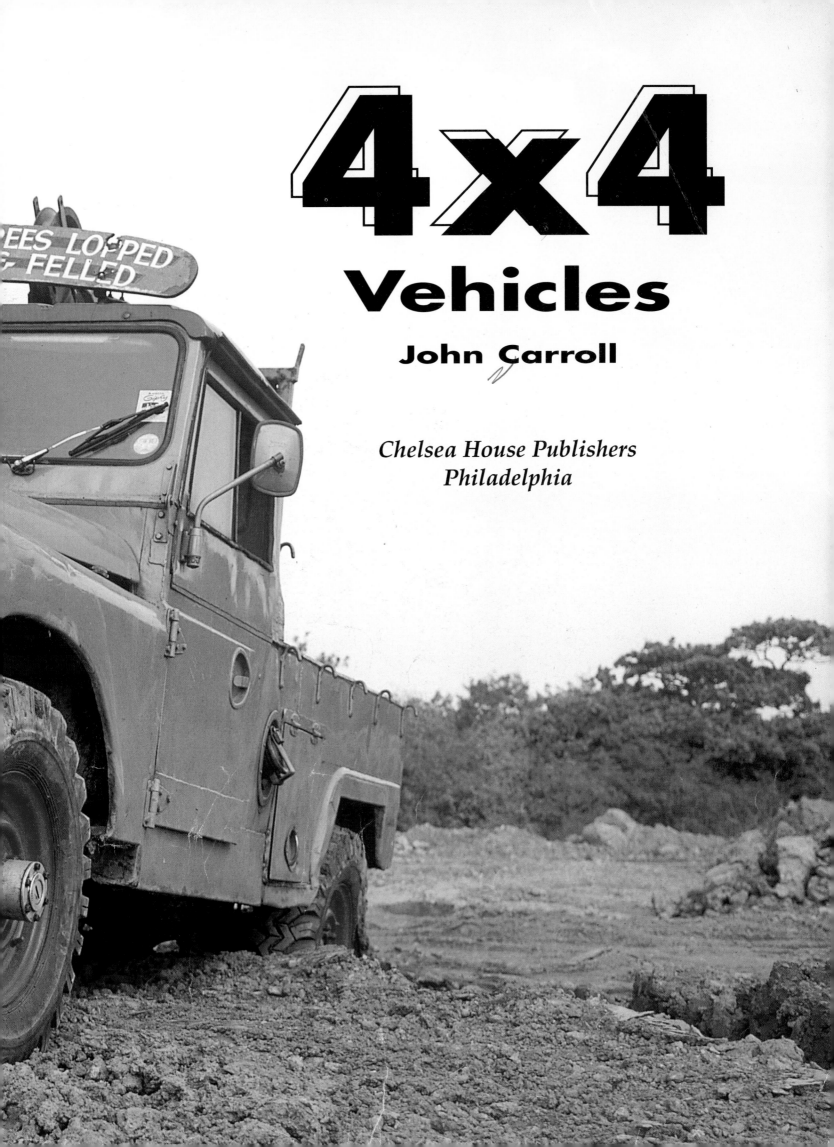

4x4

Vehicles

John Carroll

Chelsea House Publishers
Philadelphia

John Carroll has been a four-wheel-drive enthusiast since he bought his first Land Rover more than ten years ago. He currently owns a 1958 Series I Land Rover and a licence-built CJ3B Jeep, both of which feature in this book. He is a full-time motoring journalist and regularly writes for British four-wheel-drive enthusiast magazines, including *Land Rover World*. In 1991, he accompanied the British Team on the prestigious Camel Trophy event travelling in the back of the team Land Rover Discovery between Dar Es Salaam, Tanzania, and Bujumbura in Burundi.

Photography by the author, Johnathon Oakes, Ian Clegg, Richard Rawsthorn, Garry Stuart and Gareth Williams.

Pages 2-3: Kim Hallworth's hardworking Austin Gipsy 4x4

Left: Barry Redman's 1947 CJ2A Jeep

Published in 1998 by
Chelsea House Publishers
1974 Sproul Road, Suite 400, P.O. Box 914
Broomall, PA 19008-0914

Copyright © 1998
Regency House Publishing Limited

Library of Congress Cataloging-in-Publication Data applied for

ISBN 0-7910-5004-1

Printed in China

Contents

INTRODUCTION

This Willys CJ3B Jeep (above) has been modified for off-road use through the addition of aggressive tyres and the fitting of a roll cage to ensure the crew's safety in the event of it rolling over.

A surprisingly small proportion of the world's roads are surfaced, many being little more than rough tracks or lines on maps. Add to this man's need to go beyond whatever roads do exist for tasks such as defence, mineral extraction, exploration, agricultural work and forestry, not to mention plain and simple fun, and it was inevitable that, in this the age of the automobile, people would come up with cars capable of crossing the roughest of terrain. A term such as 'rough terrain' covers any number of ground conditions ranging from icy wastes to sandy deserts and impassable swamps and every imaginable combination in between as well as huge variations brought about by seasonal changes such as snows and monsoons.

From the earliest days of the auto-

mobile engineers, designers and dreamers were trying to find ways of pushing the limits of vehicles' capabilities. They required them to carry more, go faster and, of course, go further. Commercial vehicle manufacturers and military engineers in particular sought ways of getting vehicles across rough terrain and, indeed, by the time of the First World War, were having a degree of success and four-wheel-drive lorries were beginning to be both practicable and practical. But in the way the Model T Ford revolutionized both motor manufacture in particular and motoring in general it wasn't until the advent of the Willys Jeep that the small, light, general purpose and mass-produced four-wheel-drive vehicle arrived.

Since then things have never been

the same: almost every major motor manufacturer builds and sells a large-car-sized four-wheel-drive as a matter of course. Two things are particularly common in the manufacture of four-wheel-drive vehicles, namely licence-building and marketing machines in different countries with different names. The phenomenon of licence-building has been going on from the immediate postwar years when Willys licensed other companies on other continents to build their products. Vehicles are supplied by the original manufacturer as CKD – completely knocked-down – kits and assembled elsewhere or are completely produced locally. The latter option often keeps earlier style 4x4s in production where function is more important than in the more fashion conscious markets of

Europe and North America. Marketing vehicles with different names occurs for several reasons: in some markets a different model name is perceived as being more in tune with a particular market or, in the global case of multinational motor manufacturers, the same vehicle is produced not only by different plants but nominally different companies. An example of this is General Motors who produce Isuzu, Vauxhall, Opel and Holden vehicles around the world.

This book opens by considering the history and development of four-wheel-drive and takes an in-depth look at two of the first and probably the world's most famous manufacturers. It goes on to feature other machines from almost every corner of the world and explores the uses to which they are put.

The M151 MUTT – Military Utility Tactical Truck – was the U.S. Army's light 4x4 of the Vietnam War era.

CHAPTER ONE
HISTORY AND DEVELOPMENT

The Willys MB Jeep (also produced by Ford as the GPW) was the first mass-produced 4x4. It provided transport for the allied armies of the Second World War in every theatre of operations.

The first four-wheel-drive car was exhibited at the Paris Motor Show in 1903. It had been made by a Dutch company called Spijker (subsequently spelt Spyker to aid foreign sales) and designed for use on the unsurfaced roads of the Dutch Colonies. The vehicle never went into production however, and the next major development in cross-country vehicles came towards the end of the First World War when early tanks were successful. At this time, in the United States, Nash built a successful four-wheel-drive lorry which appealed to the military.

The success of tracks off-road led to the development of half-tracks, such as the vehicles from Citroën Kégresse which were proven on expeditions to Africa. French expeditions made the first Sahara desert crossing between December 1922 and January 1923. Later, another French team drove from Algeria in North Africa to the Cape of Good Hope in the south between November 1924 and July 1925. A third expedition in 1931 took French crews from Beirut to French Indo-China (now Vietnam). The British and American armies experimented with Kégresse systems and in 1923 the Americans also investigated the possibilities of wheeled vehicles off road. They used a stripped down Model T Ford that had been converted to four-wheel-drive and fitted with large tyres and found it to be a competent performer.

Elsewhere in the world people were taking two-wheel-drive cars and light commercials on journeys that pushed the limits of what was possible; overland trips around Australia, across America, up, down and across the African continent and overland from Europe to Asia were all achieved by pioneer overlanders although the journeys were nearly always extremely arduous.

In the years prior to the Second World War, Ralph Bagnold used two-wheel-drive Fords to explore much of the desert of North Africa and a lot of what he learned was passed onto the various units of the British Army who travelled the same deserts during the Second World War and established much of what is now common practice for overland travel and expedition four-wheel- drive use. It was this global conflict that accelerated the development of a practical and mass-produced light 4x4: the Japanese produced a military car in the late Thirties called a Kurogane and the Americans produced the Jeep which is detailed in a subsequent chapter.

As late as the Sixties there were still significant first journeys to be made in 4x4 vehicles. A group of people in two 4x4s – a Willys truck and a SWB Land Rover – crossed El Tapon (the stopper) in the Darién Gap, in Panama, when it was the final obstacle to the Pan-American Highway. They took almost two months to drive the 200 miles across the 'impassable' stretch of the Darién Gap on behalf of the Committee of the Pan-American Highway Congress. Later, the Range Rover would strive to cross a similar route in Darién as a promotional venture.

Four-wheel-drive systems and the engineering behind them has come a long way since a successful system was adopted by Willys-Overland in the Forties. Four-wheel-drive vehicles differ from two-wheel-drives simply because they use a different transmission system to drive two axles rather than just one. Traditional four-wheel-drive vehicles tend to use a pair of live axles that are attached to the chassis by either coil or leaf springs and to drive the differential in each axle requires a gearbox with two drive shafts, one facing the front axle and one the rear. The part of the transmission that achieves this is known as the transfer box and to allow for better gear ratios for off-road use the transfer box in most 4x4s has two speeds, high ratio and low ratio: it is the latter ratio that is used off-road. These are selected by means of an additional gear lever in many 4x4s. The terms 4x4, incidentally, is of military origin being the way vehicles are classified, the first four referring to the number of wheels a particular machine has while the second four refers to how many are driven. It is therefore equally possible to have 6x6 and 6x4 vehicles as in certain trucks.

There are two main types of four-wheel-drive systems, full-time and part-time. Full-time means that the vehicle is constantly driving all four wheels while part-time systems need four-wheel-drive selecting for difficult conditions. It was the part-time system that was widely proven first. The reason why part-time systems need drive to the second axle selecting is because of something referred to as 'wind up'. Although there are differentials in each axle there is no differential in the gearbox so both shafts turn equal numbers of revolutions. While on loose and muddy surfaces the wind up is scrubbed off but on surfaces where traction is better it is not, so the transmission tightens up as wheels rotate at different speeds when cornering. As the transmission tightens up

it will increase tyre wear, make changing gear more difficult and eventually damage the gearbox. For a permanent four-wheel-drive system to work it was necessary to devise a gearbox that would not suffer from transmission wind up.

The way this was resolved was to fit a differential device in the gearbox which would allow both drive shafts to turn at different speeds. This, however, creates its own problems because a differential means that the drive to it will go to wherever the wheels turn most easily. On a full-time four-wheel-drive system this means that it is possible to have three wheels on firm ground and one in mud spinning so that the vehicle is stuck! (the comparable situation on a selectable four-wheel-drive system is that one wheel on each axle must be spinning to be stuck). To overcome this the 'diff lock' – as the differential lock is often referred to – was developed. By means of a lever, the driver of a permanent four-wheel-drive vehicle, such as a Range Rover, can engage the diff lock which means that the centre or gearbox differential is in effect overridden, putting the machine back on a par with the part-time system as used in older Land Rovers.

The Range Rover has in recent years benefited from a viscous coupling that engages the diff lock automatically when a wheel begins to spin. To further enhance a 4x4's off-road ability, it is possible to fit locking differentials to either or both front and rear axles. Such differentials are manufactured by a number of companies around the world but relatively few 4x4s have them fitted by the manufacturers, a notable exception being the Mercedes G-Wagen and its more agricultural stablemate, the Unimog.

Part-time four-wheel-drive vehicles can benefit from another accessory – freewheeling hubs. These are devices bolted to the hubs that allow the wheel to rotate disengaged from the halfshaft which reduces vibration, fuel consumption

and wear when the vehicle is being used on surfaced roads. Some four-wheel-drive vehicles that spend time being towed on an A-frame behind another vehicle have such hubs fitted to the rear axle, too. Freewheeling hubs have to be engaged prior to driving off-road, usually by turning the end of the hub to a locked position. The Japanese manufacturers have developed an automatic freewheeling hub that is engaged when four-wheel-drive is selected and disengaged by reversing.

Although live axles – a tube that contains the differential and halfshafts – are found on many four-wheel-drive machines, it is not uncommon to see independently sprung systems. These feature a differential mounted on the chassis with unenclosed shafts running to the hubs. Steyr Puch used this system for the Haflinger and Pinzgauer vehicles. The other important factor about axle type and suspension is that, as well as guaranteeing a degree of comfort for the driver and passengers, it ensures that the wheels stay in contact with the ground – vital if traction is not to be lost. The movement of the axles over rough ground is described as axle articulation and the greater articulation an axle has the rougher the ground the vehicle can cross. This partially explains the recent trend from leaf springs to coil springs in four-wheel-drive machines with live axles.

The 4x4 has in approximately 50 years developed from a basic utility machine into a luxurious form of transport. Land Rover, who started making 4x4s aimed at farmers after the Second World War, currently produce the Discovery (right). This one is photographed in the Highlands of Scotland.

There are three other aspects of a four-wheel-drive vehicle that considerably affect its off-road performance, namely, approach, departure and ramp breakover angles. Approach angle is the angle measured from where the front wheels meet the ground to the lowest forward part of the vehicle. This angle is the steepness of obstacles that can be climbed; the departure angle is the same angle but measured at the rear of the vehicle and gives an indication of how steep an obstacle the vehicle can descend without becoming fast. On some 4x4 pickups with long rear overhangs this can be quite shallow. The ramp breakover angle is the angle to the lowest point of the vehicle at an equidistance between the axles and is used to determine how steep a hump the vehicle can drive over without becoming stuck. The shorter a vehicle's wheelbase, the higher the ramp breakover angle and the shorter its front and rear overhangs the higher its approach and departure angles. For 4x4s primarily designed to cross rough terrain these are all maximized but with vehicles designed to carry loads on unsurfaced tracks or across fields then these angles are partially compromised by the need to increase the load area through a longer wheelbase.

The technique of driving a four-wheel-drive vehicle both on- and off-road is different to that of an ordinary car. To give a 4x4 sufficient ground clearance, designers have to build them to stand tall: the wheels tend to be of 15 or 16 inches in diameter and the engine and gearbox components are mounted above the line of the axles. This means that the centre of gravity of a 4x4 is higher than a comparative car and can be turned over if cornered too hard. The manufacturers of the CJ5

Driving 4x4 vehicles in extreme conditions requires special skills such as winching and an ability to construct bridges where there are none. Crossing those bridges requires strong nerves as this potential Camel Trophy team member illustrates in a training exercise at Eastnor Castle, England, where Land Rover do much of their testing.

Jeep were embroiled in a controversy about their vehicle in the Seventies and Suzuki were later caught up in a similar wrangle about their SJ410 4x4s. While no firm conclusions were reached, most manufacturers now suggest in the owner's handbook that a 4x4 has different handling characteristics to a road car and should be driven accordingly.

Off-road driving calls for different techniques as well. Obstacles must be approached in a way that will not damage the 4x4 or cause it to become stuck on the obstacle it is crossing. However, on other occasions, momentum must be used to power a 4x4 up an incline, particularly where it is wet or slippery. Descending steep hills must be done using the engine and transmission to brake rather than the brake pedal because it is easy to lock the wheels, causing the 4x4 to slide out of control. Inclines should be ascended and descended perpendicular to the slope to prevent them being rolled over. In deep water, care must be taken to avoid damage to the 4x4 through the ingress of water into the engine, transmission and axles. With care, it is possible to ford deep water, indeed some 4x4s, particularly those used on expeditions, have a raised air intake that runs up the side of the windscreen allowing water of more than waist height to be forded.

Other aspects of off-road travel can be hazardous, too, for example, winching. The use of a winch requires a number of basic safety rules to be observed: a winch operator should wear gloves to protect his or her hands from broken wire strands and should always stand clear of a taut cable in case it snaps. The forces in a cable moving a 4x4 are such that it could badly injure or kill someone were it to snap. For this reason, no one should ever step over a taut cable. Many clubs and off-road specialists offer training in safe working practices with regards to winching, jacking and vehicle recovery.

CHAPTER TWO
THE AMERICAN JEEP

The Jeep is often referred to as a war baby because it was developed purely to satisfy the needs of the allied military during the Second World War. Since then, however, it has become one of the two most recognizable four-wheel-drive vehicles in the world, the other being the postwar Land Rover.

In June 1940, the U.S. Quartermaster Corps issued a specification for a lightweight vehicle capable of carrying men and equipment across rough terrain and invited manufacturers to build prototypes and submit them for testing. Two manufacturers showed sufficient interest to build prototypes, namely Willys-Overland and American Bantam, both of whom were in some financial difficulty at the time. Willys' prototype was late and Bantam received a contract for 70 vehicles after considerable testing of their machine – the Bantam BRC – at Camp Holabird in Maryland, U.S.A. Both Ford and Willys were given copies of the blueprints for the Bantam machine which was seen by many as the army having its doubts about Bantam's ability to build and supply its 4x4 in the numbers in which it would be required. Further contracts were issued calling for vehicles from Ford and Willys who subsequently submitted their prototypes, the Pygmy and the Quad respectively.

All three companies' machines had the early Jeep 'look'. In further testing it was revealed that all three machines had both strengths and weaknesses. Ford submitted a redesigned

prototype, the Ford GP, as did Willys, the MA. It was the Willys MA that seemed best overall after further strenuous evaluation tests and, in July 1941, Willys was given a contract for 16,000 revised MA models which were referred to as the MB. The Bantam BRC and Ford GP quickly faded into the background. Ford, who had a massive manufacturing capability, accepted a contract in November 1941 to manufacture the Willys MB to Willys specifications. The Ford-built examples were known as GPWs. So the legend of the Jeep was born and in every theatre of war

The shape of the Willys MB Jeep (above and right) was familiar to every soldier of the Second World War. The diminutive 4x4 carried soldiers forward to battle, casualties away from the fighting and did a thousand and one other jobs.

from the muddy quagmires of the Belgian Ardennes to the jungles of Burma and the sands of Iwo Jima, the Jeep endeared itself to the soldiers of the allied armies. Fighting machine, ambulance, message carrier, mechanical mule, recreational vehicle; the Willys Jeep was all of these and more. It was the transport of all ranks from privates to generals on all types of terrain.

By the end of the war General Eisenhower was to comment that the Jeep was among the foremost tools that helped America win its war, the others being the amphibious truck, Douglas DC3 aeroplane and the bulldozer. When the war ended, Willys had built 358,489 MB Jeeps and Ford had built 277,896 GPWs.

The MB/GPW in its final form had two differential equipped axles mounted to the Jeep's channel section steel chassis by semi-elliptic springs. The gearbox featured three forward and one reverse gears with a high and low ratio selected by means of an additional gear lever. A third lever enabled selection of two- or four-wheel-drive to be made. The low ratio gears could only be used in four-wheel-drive. The basic steel bodytub was bolted to the chassis, the hood was collapsible and the windscreen could be folded forwards onto the bonnet to present a lower silhouette. The interior was extremely basic and contained little more than simple seats with canvas-covered cushions to provide seating for four persons; two in the front on individual seats

The M38A1 Jeep (above) was another Jeep constructed especially for military service from which was spawned the famous CJ5.

The CJ2A (above right) was the civilian vehicle derived from the wartime MB. This particular one is from 1947 and has been modified for recreational fourwheeling, including the fitment of a front-mounted winch, alloy wheels and all-terrain tyres, as well as a Chevrolet V8 engine.

and a rear bench seat. The exterior of the vehicle had brackets to carry an axe and spade, a jerry can and a spare wheel and tyre. It has been jokingly suggested that Jeep is an acronym for 'Just Enough Essential Parts'.

A number of Jeep variants were considered and built as prototypes including a six-wheeled Jeep and a four-wheel-steering Jeep while other variants actually went into production. The best known of these latter variants was an amphibious Jeep, nicknamed the Seep. In addition to this, many Jeeps were modified for specific tasks such as transporting stretcher-borne casualties or for airborne transportation.

As the war drew to a close, it became apparent that vehicles such as the Jeep would be invaluable to farmers and ranchers, so Willys-Overland, who had the foresight to register Jeep as their trademark, began to prepare for the production of the civilian Jeep which was to be tagged CJ. Initially the Jeep CJs were marketed for agricultural purposes being equipped with power take-offs and agricultural drawbars. They were promoted through a variety of farming tasks such as towing ploughs

and disc rotators.

Other early variants included Jeeps fitted with firefighting equipment made by The Howe Fire Apparatus Company of Anderson, Indiana. The first postwar Jeep was the CJ2A which appeared on the surface to be simply a military Jeep in a different colour. But beneath the familiar exterior were revised transmission, axles and differential ratios. More obvious alterations included a hinged tailgate and relocation of the spare wheel to the vehicle's side. There were also numerous detail improvements including bigger headlights and a relocated gas cap. The engine was only slightly upgraded from the MB.

Production of the CJ2A lasted until 1949, by which time there had been 214,202 produced. This production run overlapped with the second of the CJs — the CJ3A. This Jeep went into mass production in 1948 and was continued until 1953. The main differences between the CJ2A and CJ3A were a further strengthened transmission and transfer case and a one-piece windshield. In 1953, the CJ3B was introduced with a noticeably different silhouette because of a higher bonnet line. This change was necessary

in order for Willys to fit a new engine.

The Hurricane F-head four-cylinder was a taller engine that displaced the same 134 cubic inches but produced more horsepower. The CJ3B would stay in production until the Sixties and a total of 155,494 were constructed. This model CJ would live on until the present day through a series of licensing agreements that meant it would be constructed in European, Indian and Japanese factories. Kaiser-Frazer and Willys-Overland merged in 1953 and the resulting company became known as the Kaiser-Jeep Corporation.

Another Jeep was built for the military – the M38A1 – from 1954 onwards and a civilian version was introduced the following year and tagged the CJ5. It was slightly larger than the 'flat-fenders' that had come before it as its wheelbase was one inch longer. Even though the nickname of the early models indicates that they were, its fenders, however, were not flat. The bonnet and fenders, or wings, were noticeably curved although the vehicle was still basic and featured a flat-sided design and a grille that was recognizably a Jeep. Another model appeared at the same time, the CJ6, which as simply

a longer version of the CJ5 aimed at giving commercial users a much larger load area: it had a 101-inch wheelbase compared to the 81-inch wheelbase of the CJ5.

It is generally acknowledged that the CJ5 is the model that spread the word about recreational off-road driving, especially during the Seventies when emphasis was placed on Jeeps as 'fun' vehicles. In the eyes of its customers, the CJ5 was a popular model and ensured a healthy profit for its manufacturers even though the company's car production side was loss-making and was later abandoned to enable the company to concentrate on Jeep production. A spin-off of this policy was the introduction of special Jeeps such as its forward control models and limited edition vehicles such as the 1961 Tuxedo Park. This was a CJ5 dressed up with chrome hinges, mirror supports and bumper, custom wheels and whitewall tyres and a custom hood. This model, intended for golf courses and hotels, stayed in production until 1966 albeit slightly upgraded with different paint options and better seats. Changing attitudes to off-road vehicles and rising competition from the British Land Rover and Japanese 4x4s such as the Toyota Land Cruiser and Nissan Patrol saw a V6 engine option introduced in 1966 – the Dauntless V6 – and by 1968 over 75 per cent of all Jeeps built were being supplied with this engine.

(Left) Barry Redman driving his 1947 CJ2A along The Great Ridgeway, an ancient highway that runs through the English countryside.
(Below) An impressive line-up of Jeeps on one of the Normandy, France, Invasion beaches on the 50th anniversary of D-Day.

In the front row are a variety of Ford and Willys variants including an early slat grille model and a Ford GPA amphibian. In the back row are a variety of postwar and licence-built models including an M38, a CJ2A, some Hotchkiss M201s and a Mahindra CJ340.

The American Motors Corporation –
A.M.C. – acquired Kaiser-Jeep in 1970
and introduced a V6 model in bright
orange fitted with a roll bar as standard.
For a couple of years, it pretty much left
well alone while it integrated the four-
wheel-drive models into its corporate
structure. In 1972, though, the CJ5
appeared in a much upgraded form; its
wheelbase grew in order to accommodate
the in-line 232-cubic inch six-cylinder
A.M.C. engine.

The CJ6 survived the change of ownership and its wheelbase grew to 104
inches to accommodate the new engine.
A V8 option was available using a 304-
cubic inch A.M.C. engine: this was
dropped in 1981. The Renegade

*(Right) The Jeep has endured until the
present day with its origins still obvious. The
YJ Wrangler seen here was photographed
in Hawaii. The YJ has been superseded by
the TJ which is even more recognizable as
a Jeep because of its round headlamps.*

became a regular in the Jeep line-up from
1973 with a long list of extras fitted as
standard and aimed at leisure buyers and
recreational fourwheelers.

In 1975 there was a special edition
Jeep with a Levi's denim interior. Another
engine option of the time was the four-
cylinder 151-cubic inch Iron Duke engine
that A.M.C. purchased from Pontiac. This
option which was brought about by the
second energy crisis never proved popular. More popular by far was the disc
brake upgrade firstoffered in 1977 and its
optional power assistance. Sales col-
lapsed after an American TV programme
which suggested that a CJ5 might be
liable to stability problems and easy to roll
over – a similar crisis was to embroil
Suzuki in the late Eighties. Whether true
or not, the damage was done and the
CJ5 went out of production in 1983. By
this time, a total of 603,303 CJ5s had
been built.

The CJ7 was introduced in 1976.

Longer than the CJ5, the new machine had a wheelbase of 93.4 inches and was the first Jeep to be offered with an automatic transmission option. The CJ7 was aimed squarely at recreational users and emphasis was placed on luxury with considerable amounts of chrome, more luxurious interiors and features such as air-conditioning and stereos. The most luxurious model was known as the Jeep Laredo and later the Jeep Limited. The Jeep was still a

formidable off-road machine and by the time it went out of production in 1986 379,299 had been made.

A full-time four-wheel-drive option for CJ7s with automatic transmissions was available for between1976 and 1979 and was known as Quadratrac. Although the CJ6 went out of production in 1976 an export version, the CJ6A, continued through 1981. Another commercial Jeep was the CJ8 Scrambler that featured CJ front sheetmetal combined with a truck cab and a five foot rear load bed on a chassis with a 103-inch wheelbase.

It seemed that the legend had lost some of its magic when it was announced that Jeep production would end in early 1986. There was, predictably, an outcry from loyal customers and Jeep fans who would mourn the passing of an automobile that could trace its roots back to before Pearl Harbor. However, A.M.C. had other ideas and on 13 May 1986 announced the Jeep Wrangler. The new model bore more than a passing resemblance to the old CJ series but was built taking into account any number of outside factors. Its engineers knew that a 1986 survey had discovered that only 7 per cent of Jeep owners took their vehicles off-road frequently although 80 per cent reported some off-

One of the joys of off-road vehicle ownership is the ability of the vehicle to take its driver and passengers far from the madding crowd. This Wrangler (far left and below) was photographed in one of England's National Parks on a little used trail on a summer day. The design of the Jeep grille (left) has changed only slightly in more than 50 years.

station wagon – started in 1946. It was essentially a Jeep-type grille with some chrome details fitted with pressed steel sides and mounted on a steel chassis which was also fitted with Jeep's proven engine and running gear.

Through subsequent sales years, different paint schemes, details of trim levels and advertising ploys were used – all of which ensured that the station wagon stayed in production until 1962. It was

road use. The former figure had been 37 per cent in 1978. The two statistics did not reflect a decline in off-road vehicle usage but was an indication that Jeep vehicles were appealing to a different market.

While the new machine, which was extensively tested and developed before going into production was still, at a glance, recognizable as a Jeep, it had been restyled. The restyling was most evident in the fact that the grille now featured square headlamps and was partially angled backwards. Under the body there were numerous new features including a fuel-injected 2.5-litre in-line four-cylinder or 4.2-litre in-line six-cylinder engine, a five-speed transmission with 'shift on the fly' capability and power brakes. The leaf spring suspension was set up for a decent on-road ride including front and rear track bars and

a front stabilizer bar. The interior was well appointed and the hood (on soft top models) and doors were designed to be better fitting and more waterproof. Various trim levels were available, including Sahara and Laredo specifications. The Wrangler was known as the YJ in export markets, including Canada, where the new Jeeps were assembled at the Bramalea, Ontario plant. In 1986 it became known that Chrysler was interested in acquiring A.M.C. which it subsequently did. The Wrangler is currently sold with a Chrysler Jeep badge.

Discussion of Jeep products would be far from complete without mention of the various station wagons produced by the companies who have owned the Jeep trademark over the years. Production of station wagons – America's first all-steel

replaced by the Wagoneer which, although following the same principle in being a 4x4 station wagon, was considerably more modern. The Wagoneer's basic shape remained in production until 1983. Over this period it was sold as the Cherokee, Cherokee Chief, Grand Wagoneer, among others. There were two- and four-door models and numerous engine variations including a 360-cubic inch V8. A range of interior and exterior trim levels was also offered. A new shape (once again considerably modernized) Cherokee appeared in 1984 in both two- and four-door forms.

(Above left) As well as building Jeeps, Chrysler Jeep built a range of vehicles known as Cherokees. These versatile machines offer considerable off-road performance as well as estate car-type proportions which makes them useful vehicles for official bodies such as Police Departments. The Daytona Beach, Florida Police use one to patrol the famous locale.

(Below left) Jeepers' Jamborees are off-road gatherings for enthusiastic Jeep owners to try out their vehicles away from surfaced roads. These muddy CJ Jeeps are taking part in the European Jeepers' Jamboree in France.

(Above) The usefulness of the Jeep in difficult terrain has led to its being manufactured under licence in other countries. This CJ5 was manufactured by Ford in Brazil. It was completely restored by Andrew Whitehead from England where the Jeep ended up during the Seventies.

CHAPTER THREE
THE BRITISH LAND ROVER

The roots of the Land Rover are undeniably entwined with the wartime Willys Jeep and the fact that Maurice Wilks, the Chief Engineer of the Rover Company, bought a war surplus Jeep for use on his Anglesey estate. In the early postwar years Rover, who had a reputation for building quality motor cars, was in a difficult position because of the shortage of steel and the fact that steel was allocated to companies who were producing goods for export designed to ease Britain's balance of payments situation. Rover had never been a serious exporter of its cars beyond some sales to Britain's colonies. During the war years, their Coventry factory had been blitzed and they had moved out to Solihull where they were producing items for the Air Ministry.

After seriously investigating the possibilities of producing a small aluminium-bodied car, Maurice Wilks and his brother Spencer, also a Rover employee, considered building a small utility vehicle with an aluminium body and four-wheel-drive. The intention was that the machine specifically intended for agricultural use would merely be a stopgap until sufficient steel was available for the company to return to building luxury cars. The Wilks brothers delegated much of the design work to Robert Boyle and a number of employees in the drawing office. Rover also purchased two war surplus Jeeps on which to base their design. The designers were given other criteria too: as far as possible, the Land Rover was to utilize existing

Rover components and, to avoid expensive tooling costs, the panels were to be flat or worked by hand. Unlike steel, aluminium was not rationed which was another advantage.

The first Land Rover had a tractor-like centre steering wheel to enable it to be suitable for either left- or right-hand-drive markets. Because a conventional chassis would have required expensive tooling, Olaf Poppe, an engineer, devised a jig on which four strips of flat steel could be welded together to form a box section chassis. The first prototype featured a Jeep chassis, an existing Rover car rear axle and springs, a Rover car engine and production saloon gearbox cleverly mated to a two-speed transfer box and a Jeep-like body. It was seen to have potential and an improved version was given the go-ahead in that 50 should be built for further evaluation. A larger and more powerful, but still extant, Rover car engine was fitted and the centre steering wheel was dropped.

In very nearly this form the 80-inch wheelbase vehicle was shown to the public at the 1948 Amsterdam, Holland motor show. Orders flowed in, especially when early Land Rovers were displayed at agricultural shows around Britain and the company began to look seriously at export markets. An indication of their potential was realized when, by October 1948, there were Land Rover dealerships in 68 countries. The British Army, still using Willys Jeeps and committed to the Austin

Champ as its replacement, took two Land Rovers for evaluation indicating that the new 4x4 might have uses beyond agriculture.

The first production models were different from the pilot batch in a variety of ways; some were designed to keep costs down and others to ease production or maintenance. Power take-offs and winches were an extra-cost option and between 1948 and 1954 numerous details were refined and improved. Welders and compressors were mounted aboard Land Rovers and driven by a centre PTO. An early variant was the Station Wagon which consisted of a then traditional wood framed 'shooting brake' body on a Land Rover chassis. The front wings, radiator grille and bonnet were standard Land Rover panels. While this machine was not the success it might have been, the idea was to be recycled more successfully in later years.

To make the vehicle more efficient as a load carrier it was redesigned for 1954, the wheelbase being increased by 6 inches to 86 inches and the rear overhang by 3 inches. This enabled the rear load area to be increased by 9 inches or nearly 25 per cent. A long wheelbase variant, the 107-inch was made available as a pickup and it had a huge load bed. The 86/107-inch models had a 1997cc engine which

The earliest Land Rovers went on sale in 1948 and this one (right) had an 80-inch wheelbase. They were primarily designed for agricultural use. Items like the winch were therefore useful extra-cost options.

The Land Rover's wheelbase was increased to 86 inches in 1954 and to 88 inches in 1957. The truckcab model (left) dates from 1958 and is one of the last of what became known as Series I Land Rovers. The Series II models were introduced in early 1958. Snow is one of the conditions in which four-wheel-drive vehicles are most useful (above), as illustrated by the same Series I Land Rover. From the Series I onwards, there have been long wheelbase variants of Land Rovers, this (right) is a Series III model with a wheelbase that measures 109 inches.

had been available in the latter 80-inch models. To accompany this redesign there were numerous detail improvements including a new dashboard, better door and window seals and bulkhead vents. A wider range of colours was now also on offer.

Also new for 1954 was the introduction of another station wagon designed to seat seven people, the body this time being more in keeping with the other Land Rover models and fabricated from aluminium. A long wheelbase station wagon, designed to seat ten people, was based on the 107-inch chassis. Changes were again made to the Land Rover for 1956; both models were stretched another two inches to give wheelbases of 88 and 109 inches referred to by Rover as Regular and Long

models. The extra two inches was incorporated forward of the bulkhead as Rover had new engines on the cards. The diesel engine was introduced in June 1957, its size necessitating the extra length forward of the bulkhead.

By 1958, Rover had produced in excess of 200,000 Land Rovers and it was becoming accepted that the model was more than a stopgap. It is estimated that more than 70 per cent of the Land Rovers produced had gone for export and it seems that Land Rover had worldwide market dominance in terms of lightweight 4x4s: they certainly achieved more market penetration than Jeep and by now were getting orders for military Land Rovers.

Austin, another successful British motor manufacturer, was working on a

The Ninety is the modern version of the short wheelbase Land Rover and this model (left), seen in Scotland, is a V8-engined model fitted with luxuries such as air conditioning.

The Land Rover Ninety was subsequently redesignated the Defender. Its coil springs and permanent four-wheel-drive system make it a particularly competent off-roader (above and right) as this machine, photographed in Wales, shows. Off-road driving can be hazardous and many organizations run training days where drivers can acquaint themselves with their machines.

new four-wheel-drive vehicle intended to compete with the Land Rover. It was scheduled to go into production in 1958 so, once again, Rover sought to improve its product. In April 1958, it introduced what was termed the Series II Land Rover and after this the early models were referred to as Series Is although they are commonly described by their wheelbase lengths – '80s' and '86s' – and this practice endured into later models which are described as '88s' and '109s'.

The Series II featured a redesigned body that was 1.5 inches wider than its predecessors and featured other minor improvements including more modern door hinges and bonnet latches. Soon after its introduction, the Series II was fitted with a larger engine that displaced 2286cc. Wider track axles were fitted underneath and improved suspension components gave a better ride. The idea was to update the Land Rover without changing it significantly and truck cab pickups, hardtop vans, station wagons and models with canvas tilts remained available in both wheelbase lengths.

A further upgraded model appeared in 1961, the Series IIa. Many of the changes were minimal but one of particular note was the improved diesel engine which now also displaced 2286cc. Another, to take advantage of a quirk in British law relating to motor vehicles, was to make the 109-inch station wagon a 12-seater. Great Britain wasn't the only place where legislation affected vehicle sales and a front end redesign was necessary to ensure that certain American States' laws relating to headlights were conformed to. This saw the headlamps being moved from the radiator grille panel into the fronts of the wings.

In April 1966, the 500,000th Land Rover was manufactured and while the vehicle remained essentially

unchanged until September 1971, when the Series III Land Rover was announced, there were changes elsewhere. By March 1967, Rover had become part of the British Leyland Motor Corporation. While sales of Land Rover vehicles were profitable, the corporation as a whole was not which at times had serious ramifications for the Land Rover in an increasingly competitive 4x4 market.

The Series III could be seen as Land Rover simply keeping up with the times: many of the changes were cosmetic and perceived as important to keep Land Rover vehicles up to date. There were a number of mechanical upgrades of which the most noticeable was the new all-synchromesh gearbox. This accompanied uprated brakes, clutch and rear axle on 109-inch models. The cosmetic changes included features such as a moulded plastic radiator grille and new door hinges while, inside, the dashboard was relocated in front of the driver, complete with padding, and a number of the electrical function switches were relocated onto a stalk on the steering column.

Because of their load-carrying abilities, long wheelbase Land Rovers are suitable for any number of specialist applications such as fire tenders (left) like this Series IIa employed at a small English airstrip.

Off-road driving is a popular recreational activity as evidenced by these three enthusiast-owned Land Rovers (above) on an old road in a Welsh National Park demonstrate. The activity does attract some bad press, so off-road recreational driving must to be done responsibly to avoid environmental damage.

Land Rovers have, because of their agricultural origins and reliable service, attracted large numbers of enthusiasts and early models are cherished by restorers and collectors. This 80-inch model (right) is participating in a vintage vehicle rally.

The Series III Land Rover was a popular vehicle in this (above) station wagon form where it could seat up to seven people. This particular model dates from 1983 and is therefore one of the last Series IIIs being superseded by the Ninety shortly after.

The Series III as a truckcab with a three-quarter canvas tilt (right) found favour with commercial and agricultural users because its rear load area made it a pickup truck with the versatility of a four-wheel-drive. This one is owned by a British Land Rover enthusiast who has fitted alloy wheels.

It is fair to say that Land Rover's time as part of the conglomerate was not entirely happy. Even though the millionth Land Rover was produced during this time, the company was forced to withdraw from the U.S. market and rivals were gaining a real foothold in the 4x4 market niche. There was faith in Land Rover in high places and in due course investment in the product was ensured and a V8 variant planned. The Range Rover and numerous cars used the aluminium V8 originally derived by Buick as a 215-cubic inch iron engine. The first V8 model was referred to as the Stage One and was only available in the long wheelbase models.

County models with more luxurious interiors, special paint schemes and high capacity pickups were introduced at this time but the company was already looking beyond this to the new models – the Ninety and One Ten.

So entrenched had the terms 88 and 109 become that the new models were officially designated Ninety and One Ten referring to wheelbases of 90 and 110 inches respectively. In fact, the wheelbase of the Ninety measured 92.9 inches while the One Ten's was actually 110 inches.

Unlike the other redesigns which were relatively minor the Ninety and One

Ten appeared as very different vehicles from all that had gone before but for the fact that they still looked like Land Rovers. The One Ten was unveiled at the Geneva, Switzerland Motor Show in March 1983. It featured the coil spring suspension set-up that had been used on the Range Rover since 1970.

The Range Rover came about as a result of demand for a multi-purpose 4x4 that could be both workhorse and luxury car and yet still have a high degree of off-road ability. The design and evolution of what became known as the Range Rover started in the Sixties and was based around a 100-inch wheelbase and a light-

weight V8 that Rover had obtained from a U.S. auto-manufacturer. Rather than simply being an uprated Land Rover the designers wanted to create an altogether new vehicle and so opted for both coil springs and permanent four-wheel-drive.

The final production vehicle was so unique that one was exhibited at The Louvre in Paris, rather like a piece of sculpture. It went into volume production during the early Seventies when Rover was having something of a difficult time having merged with British Leyland. The four-door Range Rover was introduced in 1981 and by 1984 was taking 90 per cent of worldwide Range Rover sales.

Export sales were always important for Range Rovers as their luxurious nature and suitability for fitting extras, such as air conditioning, made them favourites in Middle East countries. Up to 60 per cent of annual Range Rover production is exported, including a growing number to North America. A redesigned Range Rover was launched in 1994 and while it was initially marketed alongside the original-style model, the overlap of several months was purely temporary because the new one was intended to entirely supersede the original model.

The Range Rover has been described as the younger, flashier brother of the Land Rover but there has been an even younger brother in recent years, namely, the Land Rover Discovery. This was introduced at the end of the Eighties, although work had been progressing on the new machine from 1986 onwards. Mechanically, it was similar to the Range Rovers then current but in a completely different design of body and with an interior designed by Terence Conran. The vehicle featured a new diesel engine or an optional V8. The diesel engine was the one that found customers in vast numbers, particularly in Europe, when the machine went on sale in 1989.

Building on the success of the Land Rover, the company launched the Range Rover (left). It was an effective off-road vehicle with the comforts of an estate car. The mainly plastic interior was designed to be hosed out. This feature was dropped as the Range Rover became more luxurious and available in a four-door version (above). Later the company launched another luxury off-roader called the Discovery (right). Although it was a luxury machine, its four-wheel-drive capability was still excellent, as evidenced by the machine being chosen for the Camel Trophy. The five-door Discovery debuted on the 1991 Trophy, Tanzania-Burundi, and has been used ever since.

CHAPTER FOUR
THE REST OF THE WORLD

Jeeps and Land Rovers were not by any means the only four-wheel-drive vehicles manufactured around the world. Indeed, they were not even the only four-wheel-drive vehicles manufactured in their respective countries. In the United States, for example, International introduced the Scout in 1961, Ford introduced the Bronco in 1965 and Chevrolet the Blazer in early 1969. As well as these, there were numerous American-made four-wheel-drive pickups offered for sale. In Great Britain, Austin offered the main alternative to the Land Rover. They initially worked on the Champ for military contracts but later unveiled the Austin Gipsy.

This vehicle was manufactured in various guises for ten years. The Series I, announced in 1957, had a 90-inch wheelbase, was available with either petrol or diesel engines that displaced 2200cc and featured 'Flexitor' independent front and rear suspension. The Series II Gipsy appeared in 1960 with an improved independent front suspension system and a more versatile gearbox. In addition, there was a variant with a long wheelbase of 111 inches. The long wheelbase model had a conventional leaf sprung rear axle. For some reason there was no Series III and when the Series II went out of production in August 1962, its successor was the Series IV. The short wheelbase was designated GM4M10 and the long one GM4M15. The newer model was extensively restyled and leaf sprung live axles were available front and rear on all mod-

els. The Flexitor system was dropped entirely in 1965. After both Austin and Rover's amalgamation into the British Leyland Motor Corporation, the Gipsy was phased out in 1968 while Rover's Land Rover stayed in production.

It was, however, elsewhere in the world – most notably Japan – that real innovation was taking place in the production of light four-wheel-drive vehicles. Mitsubishi, Nissan and Toyota all started to produce light four-wheel-drives in the early Fifties. Mitsubishi Heavy Industries Limited entered into an agreement with Willys whereby it would build Jeeps under licence and commenced producing CJ3Bs which were redesignated Mitsubishi J3. From this they developed a range of Jeep-like vehicles including steel bodied station wagons.

Nissan introduced their first four-by-four in 1948. Clearly it had its roots in the U.S. Jeep being an open-bodied flat fender-type vehicle but Nissan called it the Patrol 4W60. It was powered by a 3670cc six-cylinder sidevalve engine and had a wheelbase that measured 86.5 inches. The name Patrol is still used by Nissan.

Toyota's entry to the four-wheel-drive market was similar to that of Nissan. It produced a Jeep-like vehicle, the Model BJ, almost at the same time, although during the war it had worked on a project for the Japanese military. Like Nissan, the new Toyota, too, had a six-cylinder engine, displacing 3386cc. The wheel

The Austin Gipsy (above) was a steel-bodied British competitor to the Land Rover. Early models had an unusual suspension arrangement but Austin and Rover's merger into British Leyland killed it off because the conglomerate did not wish to produce two competing vehicles.

and there were four different body types: the 240 – a canvas-topped pickup, the 242 – a closed cab pickup, the 243 – a van-bodied machine and the 244 – a station wagon. The type of engine fitted depended on the market for which the machines were destined, both Peugeot diesel engines and ARO petrol engines having been used. The ARO 240 models were completely basic and utterly traditional. Later production of the same vehicles was commenced in Portugal where they were known as the Portaro 260 series and fitted with Daihatsu diesel engines.

The ARO concern also produced the ARO 10S which was sold in certain export markets as the Dacia Duster. This diminutive machine is powered by a 1397cc engine and has independent front suspension and a leaf sprung rear axle. It uses some Renault components as a result of ARO's cooperation with the French company.

Auverland A3

The A3 is a very capable off-road vehicle produced in France by Auverland SA and supplied to both civil and military customers. It has a coil spring suspension set-up and a 1905cc Peugeot diesel engine and a five-speed gearbox from the same manufacturer. The transfer box is of Auverland's own manufacture. The A3 is based on a box section chassis and features a body largely made from galvanized steel.

base was approximately 90 inches and the open-, steel-bodied vehicle was clearly patterned on the U.S. Jeep. By the end of the Fifties, Toyota would have coined the name Land Cruiser that has endured to this day. The other large Japanese manufacturers, such as Suzuki, Daihatsu and Isuzu, entered the market much later.

ARO 4x4s

The Romanian state-owned automobile factory is at Cîmpulung, Romania and started producing 4x4s in 1964 through licence production of the Russian GAZ-69. In 1970, the company began production of the ARO 240 Series. These vehicles were exported from 1972 onwards

Daihatsu 4x4s

Daihatsu of Ikeda City, Osaka, Japan introduced the F10 'Taft' in 1974. It was a very basic off-road vehicle with a 958cc four-cylinder engine and a four-speed gearbox with a two-speed transfer box. Four- and six-seat versions were available. The F20 series followed in 1977 with a choice of soft or hard tops, a choice of a 1600cc petrol or 2530cc diesel engine and a choice of short or long wheelbase. The vehicle was steel-bodied and a completely traditional 4x4 with a wheelbase of almost 80 inches for the short wheelbase variant. Another restyle followed in 1983 and the vehicles that sold around the world designated the F80 and known as the Rocky or Fourtrak were announced. The F80 remained a serious and traditional off-road machine with leaf springs and live axles. A part-time 4x4 system and four-speed transmission with high and low ratios was standard equipment along with a choice of either a 1998cc petrol engine or 2765cc diesel. A soft top variant was designated the F70 and was mechanically similar.

The Daihatsu Fourtrak (left) is typical of many Japanese 4x4s in that it is conventional in terms of its chassis design, suspension and transmission system. It is powered by a turbo diesel engine and one of a plethora of popular Japanese models. The ARO 10 (above) was marketed in Britain as the Dacia Duster. Made in Romania, it uses a number of Renault components in its construction. The Auverland (right) is a French-built off-roader that is renowned for its excellent off-road performance; it is powered by a diesel Peugeot engine.

As the fashion for sport-styled 4x4s grew, Daihatsu entered the market in 1989 with the Sportrak, also known as the Feroza. This was an 85.6-inch wheelbase machine and still fairly traditional underneath with a taper leaf spring suspended rear axle complementing an independent double wishbone set-up at the front. A 1589cc alloy engine and five-speed gearbox drive a part-time four-wheel-drive system through a two-speed transfer case.

Fiat 4x4s

Fiat of Turin, Italy is a well known European motor manufacturer and has, over the postwar years, produced light 4x4s for the Italian Army. The first of these was the Jeep-like AR-59 which went into production in 1951. This was followed by the Fiat Campagnola which went into production in 1974. This is available in two wheelbases in a variety of body types such as canvas tops and station wagons with petrol or diesel engines.

More recently, in the early Eighties, Fiat launched a four-wheel-drive version of one of its smallest passenger cars. The four-wheel-drive system was developed by the Austrian company, Steyr-Puch. The normal Panda is a transverse-engined front-wheel-drive machine and the four-wheel-drive system complements this through the addition of a leaf sprung rear axle. The Panda 4x4 was also available in a limited Sisley edition.

GAZ-69

The Gorky motor factory – Gorkovsky Automobilni Zavod (GAZ) – in the former U.S.S.R. produced the GAZ-67 from 1942 onwards for the Russian Army. The GAZ-67 was superseded in 1952 by the GAZ-69 which was produced in huge numbers for Warsaw Pact countries and was subsequently assembled in certain other countries, including Korea and Romania. The vehicle is entirely traditional being based around a steel ladder frame chassis on which are hung two leaf sprung axles with a wheelbase of 90 inches. A four-cylinder petrol engine and three-speed gearbox and two-speed transfer box are fitted and the body is made from steel, a canvas tilt forming the roof. Production was also undertaken at Ulyanovsk from 1956 and the models built there were given the designation UAZ-69.

Isuzu 4x4s

Isuzu is based in Tokyo, Japan and in 1967 they introduced a two-wheel-drive

field car called the Unicab KR80. This soon diversified into true off-road vehicles of which the best known is a 4x4 station wagon which is available in two wheelbases. Like several other manufacturers' 4x4s, it is sold and manufactured around the world under a variety of names, including Trooper, Bighorn, Monterey, Passport, Jackaroo and Rodeo. There have also been commercial variants and a soft top model. The 1988 model specification included independent front double wishbone torsion bar suspension with a more traditional leaf sprung axle at the rear. Disc brakes were fitted front and rear and the suspension was mounted to a steel ladder frame chassis. Both diesel- and petrol-engined variants were manufactured. The vehicle was redesigned for the Nineties and featured a coil sprung rear axle and a range of newer engines. Alongside the production of this model around the world is sold a sport utility 4x4 variously known as the Isuzu Amigo and Rodeo, Opel and Vauxhall Frontera.

Fiat normally concentrates on building ordinary road-going cars but combined with the Austrian company, Steyr-Puch, to build a four-wheel-drive variant of their smallest saloon car. The four-wheel-drive system is part-time, selected when conditions are difficult such as in snow. This model (above) is a limited edition Sisley model and was photographed in front of a Scottish castle. The Isuzu Trooper (above right) is sold around the world under a variety of badges and names. It is a conventional Japanese off-roader while the Lada Niva (below right) is less so. The Niva is a Russian-built 4x4 based on monocoque construction and featuring permanent four-wheel-drive.

Lada Niva

The Lada Niva is officially designated the VAZ-2121, the VAZ prefix indicating that it is built at the Volzhky Automobilni Zavod in Togliattigrad in the former U.S.S.R. The company produces licence-built Fiat cars but the Niva is an all-Soviet design. It features a monocoque shell, unlike the majority of off-road vehicles which rely on a separate chassis, and features a full-time four-wheel-drive system and coil spring suspension back and front. It is powered by a 1569cc petrol engine and is a competent off-road performer, partially because of its 87-inch wheelbase.

Mercedes-Benz G-Wagen

G-wagen is an abbreviated version of Gelandewagen and the vehicle bearing this name is a prestigious and luxurious 4x4 which still manages to be incredibly capable off-road. The design is traditional and engineered to a high standard with a variety of engine options available. The live axles are coil sprung and mounted on a box section chassis and the vehicle's off-road performance is enhanced by the provision of differential locks.

Mitsubishi 4x4s

While the Tokyo, Japan-based manufacturer continued to make CJ3B Jeeps and derivatives for its home market, in particular, it launched a new 4x4 for the world market in 1981. The new machine was known by different names in different countries but Pajero and Shogun seem to have been widely used, particularly in Europe, and Montero in the United States. Its boxy shape was modern and both petrol- and diesel-engined variants were available. The new model was relatively traditional in that it featured a steel ladder frame chassis and a part-time four-wheel-drive system although new technology appeared in the form of front disc brakes, independent front suspension, automatic freewheeling hubs and a five-speed transmission.

The next generation of Mitsubishi 4x4s was announced in 1991 and was known by the same names. The bodywork was considerably redesigned and the suspension was upgraded to coil springs all round; the axle track was widened and disc brakes were fitted to both front and rear axles as well as braking being further uprated by the incorporation of ABS.

The chassis was redesigned to accept these new components and the vehicle increased in size overall. Much of the restyled bodywork was not a surprise when it appeared because, for several years, Mitsubishi had been campaigning a similar shape vehicle in the 'proto' class of the legendary Paris-Dakar desert race. This event had been supported by Mitsubishi for several years with vehicles and victories in several classes.

Mitsubishi build four-wheel-drive vehicles that are sold under different names in different countries. The Pajero, Montero and Shogun are three of these names and the box-shaped model (below) was superseded by the more rounded version (right) seen here in the Scottish Highlands in 1991.

Nissan Patrol

In 1965, Nissan of Tokyo, Japan unveiled the 4W65 Station Wagon which looked remarkably like the Willys-Overland station wagon and had all-steel bodywork and seated eight people. It was completely conventional using a 3956cc 105 bhp in-line six-cylinder engine that drove through a four-speed gearbox with high and low ratio to two leaf sprung live axles.

Soon after this followed the L60 Patrol which, although more Jeep-like in concept, had an identity all its own. It was produced throughout the Sixties and early Seventies and was only gradually updated and improved. There were soft top versions that featured folding windscreens and hard top station wagons in three wheelbases. The vehicle was steel bodied, angular and functional. The engine was a six-cylinder unit and transmission a three-speed with a two-speed transfer box, all based on a welded steel box section chassis and leaf sprung live axles. In 1980, the Patrol was relaunched in a redesigned form: once again there was a choice of wheelbase lengths and roof configurations. Since then, as the popularity of four-wheel-drive vehicles has increased exponentially it has been redesigned and face-lifted again. Nissan has also added to its range with other 4x4s such as the Nissan Pathfinder and the Spanish-built Nissan Terrano II which is also sold in some countries as the Ford Maverick.

Peugeot Dangel

While Peugeot itself do not manufacture a four-wheel-drive vehicle (with the exception of the military P4, a G-Wagen derivative) it does have an agreement with Automobilier Dangel of Sentheim, France, who manufacture four-wheel-drive conversions for the Peugeot 504 range of cars and commercials. The conversion consists of a Dangel transfer box, axles with limited slip differentials, enhanced ground clearance and underbody protection.

Rocsta

Asia Motors is based in Korea and was founded in 1965. It has produced a number of commercial vehicles and a light 4x4 known as the Rocsta. The small Jeep-like machine is available with either petrol or diesel engines and hard or soft tops. Asia Motors exports its products – including the Rocsta – to over 100 countries worldwide. There are two other up-and-coming Korean four-wheel-drive manufacturers, namely Kia and SsangYong, who produce the Sportage and the Musso respectively, both of which are luxury 4x4s.

Nissan is another of the larger Japanese 4x4 manufacturers and its Patrol models have been sold all over the world since their introduction in 1965. This one (left) was photographed in New Zealand. Korean company, Asia Motors, introduced the Rocsta (above) to European markets during the Nineties. It is a light jeep-like 4x4 and completely conventional in design. Peugeot of France has an arrangement with the Dangel company to offer 4x4 conversions to its estate cars and pickup trucks such as this 504 model (right).

Suzuki 4x4

In April 1970, a vehicle called the Jimny 360 went on sale in Japan. It was powered by an air-cooled 359cc two-stroke engine. It was both traditional in terms of its transmission and suspension layouts and basic in the extreme. It was based on the Hope Star ON360 that had been developed and briefly marketed by the Hope Motor Company which was earlier acquired by Suzuki of Hamamatsu, Japan, in 1968. An early export market for the Jimny was Australia where customers were soon clamouring for similar vehicles but with larger engines. So a model was marketed with a three-cylinder 550cc water-cooled engine and subsequently a four-cylinder four-stroke that displaced 797cc. This latter vehicle was known as the LJ80.

In 1980 Suzuki introduced a new model, the SJ Series, that featured a redesigned chassis, new axles and a 970cc four-cylinder engine. It was slightly longer than the LJ and featured a redesigned chassis, new axles and a redesigned bodyshell. In the years since, there have been any number of variants including soft tops, hard tops, commercial vans, a variety of wheelbases, licence-built models (most notably in Spain by Santana SA after 1982) and even a long wheelbased closed cab pickup. Later came the SJ413 with a 1324cc engine and wider track axles but otherwise very similar. Altogether different was the new Suzuki, introduced in 1988, featuring a more sport-styled body, coil spring suspension and a 1.6-litre engine. It is called the Vitara in the United Kingdom, the Escudo in Japan and the Sidekick and Geo Tracker in the U.S.A.

The SJ series of Suzuki 4x4s (left) has proved tremendously popular right around the globe. This one is a soft top commercial variant photographed on an old unsurfaced route among the mountains of the English Lake District. The flat-fendered Toyota Land Cruiser (below) is a common sight the world over and has a reputation for being a tough and reliable workhorse. It was offered in a variety of wheelbases and body configurations.

Toyota Land Cruiser

From the humble beginnings of the BJ models, Toyota's four-wheel-drive vehicles progressed rapidly. The name Land Cruiser has been in continuous use by the Nagoya, Japan-based concern since it first appeared on the completely restyled version of the BJ which was referred to as the FJ series. These models still bore a resemblance to the Jeep with flat wings and a flat windscreen but soon evolved into Toyota's own businesslike vehicle which rapidly found favour in export markets such as Asia and Africa. As a result, the vehicles are numerous and have earned themselves a good reputation.

Since the Sixties, there have been any number of FJ-series variants in a variety of wheelbases ranging from short wheelbase station wagons to long wheelbase pickups. More recently, there have been differing Toyota models that still bear the Land Cruiser name being produced at the same time for mainly different but sometimes overlapping markets. On the whole, the Toyota has stayed true to the idea of leaf sprung axles on a sturdy ladder chassis but its most recent, and most luxurious models, such as the Land Cruiser VX and Land Cruiser II, feature coil springs. Toyota has built numerous other four-wheel-drive vehicles such as an estate car with 4x4 capability marketed in some places as the Tercel, with larger machines such as the 4Runner and the sport utility the RAV4.

The name Land Cruiser has been given to a number of different models of Toyota 4x4s including these large station wagons (below) photographed in the sand dunes of Dubai, one of the States that borders the Persian Gulf.

The UMM (above right) is a utility 4x4 manufactured in Portugal. It is a competent machine and contemporary versions are powered by Turbo diesel engines.

Licence-building is common among four-wheel-drive vehicles; the two vehicles (below right) are licence-built machines; in the foreground is a Mahindra CJ340, which is an Indian licence-built CJ3B Willys jeep, while in the background is a Santana SJ410, a Spanish-built Suzuki SJ410.

UMM Alter

UMM – Uniao Metalo Mecanica – is based in Lisbon, Portugal and produces the UMM Alter which has also been marketed as both a Dakary and a Transcat. It is a basic machine aimed primarily at a strictly utility market. A variety of body configurations of this angular machine are available as are diesel and petrol engines. UMM exports a percentage of its production.

Licence-Building

This is a phenomenon that is not exclusive to four-wheel-drive manufacture but is certainly common and has been the norm since the mass production of the Willys Jeep. In order to reach the volume production of Jeeps necessary for the allied armies in the Second World War, Ford built the Willys product in its factories. After the war, Willys, and the later owners of that trademark, lost no time in arranging licensing agreements with numerous manufacturers to allow them to built Jeeps. Mitsubishi of Japan, Mahindra of India, Hotchkiss of France, Ford of Brazil, Nekaf of Holland, Ebro and Viasa of Spain, Bravia of Portugal and Ford of Canada are just some of the motor manufacturers who have built either CKD kits or locally produced Jeeps. A large number of countries built CJ3B models and a lesser number CJ5s. A further twist has been that some of these licence-builders have themselves supplied CKD kits for assembly elsewhere. An example of this is Mahindra and Mahindra of Bombay, India who have supplied CKD CJ3B kits for final assembly in Iran. Mahindra also produced the only CJ4 models to have been so designated.

Some of the licence-builders have concentrated on producing Jeeps for the armies of their respective countries. Hotchkiss produced thousands of slightly updated Willys MBs known as the M-201, for the French Army, while Nekaf produced M38A1 models for the Dutch army. Another quirk of licence-building is that it keeps older style vehicles in production, often long after they have been discontinued by their original manufacturer thus creating unlikely export markets. Mahindra, for example, export their CJ3B to most European countries where it sells to those who want a basic no-frills off-road vehicle.

Land Rovers, too, have been licence-built by several companies, including Minerva of Belgium, who produced a Land Rover Series I with slightly restyled front wings for the Belgian Army and Tempo of Germany who built something similar. The most famous licence-builder of Land Rovers, though, is Santana SA of Spain who built a variety of Land Rover vehicles, including short and long wheelbase models and some that were never available in the UK. Santana went on to build SJ series Suzukis in huge numbers. The SJ Suzukis were also built in India as Marutis while the Nissan Patrol has been built in the same country as the Jonga and in Spain by Ebro. Toyota FJ-series Land Cruisers are built in Brazil where Toyota built an assembly plant in São Paulo in the Fifties. In Brazil, the Land Cruiser is sold as the Bandeirante and powered by a Mercedes diesel engine. Zastava of Kragujevac, in the former Yugoslavia, manufactured the Fiat AR-59 as the Zastava AR-51.

Although Mahindra build Willys Jeeps under licence, they also produce derivatives of their own. This machine, referred to as an MM (above and right), is basically a Jeep in that its chassis and running gear are the same as the licence-built models; but its bodywork is of Indian design despite its similarity to a CJ5.

CHAPTER FIVE
COMMERCIAL FOUR-WHEEL-DRIVE

America can be described as the land of the pickup truck, such is that versatile vehicle's popularity, and with four-wheel-drive that versatility is further increased. Willys was among the first to see the advantages that four-wheel-drive would offer a great number of commercial vehicle users and so offered a range of four-wheel-drive pickups alongside their Jeeps. The trucks differed from Jeeps but the design of their grille and front wings left no doubt as to which company had designed and manufactured them. The pickup trucks featured a closed cab with a variety of rear body types being available including a stepside, a stake bed and a chassis cab for specialist equipment to be installed on the back. The pickup range was complemented by a line of -panel vans and an estate car line.

The four-wheel-drive models were capable of mounting power take-offs to drive machinery. The first 4x4 truck from Willys rolled off the Toledo, Ohio production line in February 1948 and trucks continued to do so until 1963, with only minor improvements along the way. The grille was slightly redesigned and a one-piece windscreen substituted for the two-piece item originally used.

Until the Fifties, though, 4x4 pickups from the major U.S. manufacturers were something of a novelty; International Harvester introduced their first 4x4 pickup in 1953 with the R-series. In late 1955 they, then the third largest pickup truck

manufacturer in the United States, brought out the S-series of trucks, including the S-120 4x4. There were 13 variations of this truck with four different wheelbases, chassis-cabs, stake beds, platform trucks.

Ford, GMC and Chevrolet also offered 4x4 trucks, usually a four- wheel-drive variant of an existing truck; for example, Ford's first contenders for the growing market were the 1956 F-100 and F-250 4x4 models available as pickups and chassis cabs.

Dodge built a really serious 4x4 working truck during the Fifties based on a mili-

tary vehicle they had supplied to America's services during the Second World War. It was known as the Power Wagon and was the undisputed king off the highway in America's backwoods. It was used for logging and oil exploration and wilderness projects such as dam construction. There were Power Wagons with a variety of bodies and all were built by Chrysler's Dodge Truck Division and briefly marketed under the De Soto and Fargo names. The Power Wagon spawned a whole range of heavy duty 4x4s including the Chevy and GMC Suburbans and Crew Cabs.

Four-wheel-drive vehicles have long been popular for commercial applications. This Forward Control Willys truck (left) was a way of increasing a vehicle's load area while retaining a relatively short wheelbase. The 4x4 Chevy pickup (above) is a popular vehicle in the United States and often customized, like this one photographed in Wyoming. It has been fitted with a roll bar, larger wheels and tyres and a number of KC Daylighter spotlights.

Forward Controls

Another type of 4x4 created especially for commercial use was the forward control type. The idea behind these machines was that by putting the cab over the front axle and engine it created a larger load bed while still retaining a relatively short wheelbase. Such vehicles were built by both Jeep and Land Rover. The Jeep models were first introduced in 1957 and stayed in production for seven years. There were two models, the FC-150 and FC-170. The FC prefix clearly stands for forward control and the numerical desig-

nation refers to the wheelbase. The FC-150 was based around the 81-inch wheelbase of the CJ5, then in production, while the FC-170 was based on a 103.5-inch wheelbase chassis. The short model had a four-cylinder engine and the longer one a six. The remainder of the machines were similar, both utilizing leaf sprung axles, drum brakes, two-speed transfer boxes and three-speed gearboxes.

Land Rover, too, used an existing chassis on which to base their Forward Control model, that of the 109-inch Land Rover. They also incorporated the four-cylinder 2286cc engine. The first of these forward controls was shown to the public in 1962 and this model stayed in production until 1966. The revamped version appeared with a choice of diesel or six-cylinder petrol engine and a slightly lengthened chassis and wider axles. In this form, Land Rover's Forward Control endured until the early Seventies. Both Jeep and Land Rover forward control models found favour in export markets and for specialist use, such as conversions into fire appliances.

U.S. 4x4 Pickups

In the mid-Sixties, the huge American motor manufacturers introduced 4x4 pickups that were available in fleetside and stepside body types and were essentially upgraded versions of their two-wheel drive models. These were vehicles such as the Chevrolet K-series, Ford F-series and GMC trucks and they spawned a number of sport-utility 4x4s such as the Chevy Blazer, GMC Jimmy, Ford Bronco, Dodge Ramcharger, and International Scout.

The Bronco was an early trend-setter and was the first truly mass-marketed 4x4 in the U.S.A. The model was introduced late in 1965 for the 1966 sales year and was available in three versions – open-

bodied roadster, sport utility and enclosed wagon. It featured innovative coil spring suspension and an in-line six-cylinder engine with a V8 as an option. They were fairly basic, options such as power steering and automatic transmissions not being available until 1973. The Bronco lasted in almost its original guise until 1977 when it was replaced by the bigger Bronco which was based on a Ford F-150 pickup chassis and became closer in concept to the Chevy Blazer. The more modern Bronco II is perhaps closer to the original Bronco concept.

Chevrolet's Blazer was the first of the full size, big-engined vehicles based on the idea of a shortened 4x4 pickup chassis. It first appeared during the 1969 model year in both six- and eight-cylinder engine types and was designed to use existing and proven Chevy/GMC light truck components that would ensure it gained market place credibility. The GMC Jimmy appeared in 1970 and was virtually identical to the Chevrolet Blazer except for some trim parts. The highest specification Blazer until 1973 was the CST – Custom Sport Truck – and the Cheyenne specification package was introduced in 1973, a roll bar becoming standard in 1975. All the 4x4 models were leaf sprung front and rear.

International Harvester introduced their range of 4x4 pickups in the early Fifties and manufactured them for many years. This one (left) is a 1956 S-120 model that still earns its keep in South Dakota. The Dodge Power Wagon (above) was a strictly utility 4x4 truck. This example was photographed in Wyoming where it had spent many years being used on fencing work. The Chevrolet stepside 4x4 (right) was built in 1979 although it has been modified with the fitting of a lift kit to accommodate 44.18.5.15 Gumbo Monster Mudder tyres. These aggressive tyres are ideal for a 4x4 used in muddy conditions.

Toyota HiLux

This vehicle is probably one of the all-time top ten 4x4s, despite its relatively recent introduction. In the United States, where recreational four-wheeling was a massively growing sport, despite the gas crisis of 1979-80, the acceptance that the Japanese manufacturers *did* offer a quality product meant that, in 1979, when Toyota first introduced the HiLux pickup, it found eager buyers. Prior to this, there had been independent attempts to convert two-wheel drive Japanese pickups into 4x4s and this had further fuelled the market demands. It soon became apparent that the new truck could do anything a CJ Jeep could do despite its smaller engine.

The first Toyota HiLuxes were fitted with an in-line four-cylinder engine of relatively small displacement but sufficient to perform well and deliver reasonable fuel

economy. Off the tarmac the truck was proving popular and recreational users began to customize their machines with roll bars and bigger wheels and tyres, suspension lift kits, winches and any number of other truck accessories. Suddenly, a whole new genre of off-road vehicles had arrived and soon spread beyond the U.S.A.

The other Japanese manufacturers, including Nissan, Isuzu and Mitsubishi, soon introduced 4x4 pickups. The current model from Mitsubishi sells around the world under a variety of names, including Triton, Mighty Max and L200. Even commercial 4x4s are built under licence and for a time Volkswagen built the long-running Toyota HiLux pickup and sold it in Europe as a VW Taro.

The HiLux has been extensively upgraded in its 15-year history, the body has become smoother over the years and the

suspension has been upgraded from leaf springs to coils. In the United States, the new generation of Toyota trucks are referred to as Tacomas and assembled in Fremont, California.

Forward Control 4x4s such as this Land Rover (above) were suited to specialist conversions. This particular machine was converted to a fire engine for an Isle of Man fire brigade through the fitment of a completely coach-built rear body as well as the installation of specialist fire-fighting equipment.

Toyota offer this pickup (above right) based on their Land Cruiser chassis and cab. This one was in use in Dubai where the four-wheel-drive capability is useful in the sand dunes.

The Forest Rover (below right) was an early Sixties conversion to a Land Rover by Roadless Traction Limited to make the vehicle suitable for forestry work. The conversion required special wider axles in order to fit the 10x28 wheels and open centre tyres. This particular machine is now preserved by the Dunsfold Land Rover Trust in England.

Almost all the Japanese manufacturers offer a four-wheel-drive pickup truck. This Nissan 4x4 (top left) is in use in California while the Isuzu (top right) is sold in England as the Vauxhall Brava. The Toyota HiLux is probably the best known of the Japanese four-wheel-drive pickups and has been in production ifor more than 15 years, although it has been redesigned and upgraded in this time. It is possible to get any 4x4 stuck, especially in the sea (left). The larger vehicle about to come to its rescue is a GMC 6x6 DUKW amphibian, built for the U.S. Army during the Second World War, although this particular one is still in use by the lifeguards on a Southport, England beach.

CHAPTER SIX
MILITARY
FOUR-WHEEL-DRIVE

The world's armed forces, armies in particular, have two requirements of four-wheel-drive vehicles; first, they require them as transport for men and supplies in difficult terrain and second, and perhaps less frequently, they require their four-wheel-drive vehicles to be actual fighting machines. As a result of these requirements, some four-wheel-drive vehicles have been built specifically for military contracts while other civilian vehicles are modified to fulfil military roles. Because of the nature of war, armies often have to move considerable amounts of men, equipment and supplies across the roadless terrain of battlefields and on many occasions across areas where roads and tracks have been destroyed by fighting. Consequently, modern armies usually employ four-wheel-drive vehicles ranging from the smallest Land Rover to the largest truck.

As in so many other areas of four-wheel-drive vehicles, the Willys Jeep was the first to fit military needs and, as has already been pointed out, came about specifically for a military contract. It supplied transport in every theatre of operations during the Second World War and was, on occasions converted into a fighting vehicle. One famous example is the way Jeeps were put to use by the British SAS in the deserts of North Africa. Machine guns were mounted on the Jeeps which were stripped of roofs and windscreens and loaded with supplies.

Jeep-borne patrols mounted raids

The Willys Jeep (below) was mass-produced for the allied military of the Second World War. Its off-road performance was phenomenal and the machine soon became a legend, unlike the Austin Champ (below right). The Champ was a British-designed and built 4x4, intended for military use, but its advanced engineering features and heavy weight meant that the simpler and lighter Land Rover was more suited to military applications.

behind German lines and the vehicle also saw service in subsequent wars, including Korea and Vietnam. The rather more recent Gulf War was in fact the first war since the Second World War that involved the U.S. Army in which they did not use Jeeps of any type. The Hummer has now succeeded the Jeep as an all-purpose military 4x4.

A number of the light 4x4s manufactured around the world were originally built for military usage, including the GAZ-69, which was for many years the main light 4x4 used by the eastern bloc armies. The Hotchkiss licence-built Jeeps and the light 4x4s built by Toyota and Fiat were used by the armies of the respective countries. Once the German army was permitted to re-equip following the Second World War it, too, needed a light 4x4 and eventually adopted a vehicle manufactured by Auto-Union and known as the Munga – an acronym for Mehrzweck Universal Gelandewagen mit Allradantrieb.

It was initially introduced in 1955 as one of three prototypes of cross-country cars for the Bundeswehr. The other models were submitted by Porsche and Goliath. After considerable testing it went into volume production in late 1956. In many ways it was an unusual vehicle because of its use of a three-cylinder two-stroke engine, permanent four-wheel-drive and identical independent suspension both front and rear. Over its lengthy production run a number of variants were produced that included slightly more powerful engines in later models.

Steyr-Puch

Two other vehicles that were produced by a European manufacturer with military service in mind were the Haflinger and Pinzgauer. Like the Munga, they are less conventional in their design than might be expected, both being products of Steyr-Puch, an Austrian concern. The Haflinger, named after a breed of

The GAZ-69 (left) became the standard light 4x4 for much of the Eastern Bloc's forces and was built in several countries, including the former U.S.S.R., Romania and Korea. This particular GAZ-69 saw service with the Polish Army. The Steyr-Puch Pinzgauers (above) were developed by the Austrian company for their own army but also sold to other friendly nations, too. Those seen here are owned by a group of enthusiasts of this versatile 4x4 vehicle.

Austrian horse, first went into production in 1959. The body is an open platform which is mounted onto a chassis that is comprises a single backbone tube onto which lockable differentials are mounted; to these are fitted independently sprung axles. A flat-twin configuration engine powers the machine which has four forward gears (this was later uprated to five forward gears). The Pinzgauer, also named after a breed of Austrian horse, is built along similar lines but is considerably larger than the Haflinger. The Pinzgauer appeared in 1971 and was designated model 710. Later, a six-

wheel-drive version was produced and designated Model 712. The Pinzgauer uses an in-line air-cooled four-cylinder engine displacing 2.5 litres. It has a two-speed transfer box and five-speed gearbox and differential locks. The Steyr-Puch products have seen service with armies as far apart as Switzerland and Australia.

The Swedish manufacturer, Volvo, also built some military 4x4 vehicles including, in the Fifties, the Sugga, a command car, and, through the Sixties, the Laplander, a forward control design of 4x4.

M151 Mutt

The Mutt is another vehicle built exclusively for the U.S. Army – the name is an acronym of Military Utility Tactical Truck – and because of its unusual rear suspension set-up has never been sold in large numbers when surplus. Instead they are scrapped by the Army and very few are consequently owned by either military vehicle or four-wheel-drive enthusiasts.

The Mutt came into being when it was realized that a successor for the M38 and M38A1 models of Jeep would be required. The Ordnance Tank Automotive Command started research into a new vehicle in 1950 and in 1951 gave the Ford Motor Company a contract to undertake a study of the concept. The prototypes that Ford built were extensively tested and in 1959 the company was given a production contract for what was designated the M151 since when, Kaiser-Jeep and their successors have built the M151, too. It was powered by an overhead valve four-cylinder engine and has four forward gears and a single-speed transfer box. Suspension was by coil springs, the rear being of a swing-axle design.

This was modified in 1964, when the Mutt became the M151A1 and, after a number of accidents, changed to a trailing arm arrangement in 1970 when it became the M151A2.

The Mutt saw extensive service in Vietnam and other variants included the M151A1C which toted a recoilless rifle: the M718A1 was an ambulance Mutt. In Tournes, France, a company called Poncin market a civilian version of the Mutt.

Military Land Rover

The Land Rover went into service with the British Army in time to see action in the Korean War. Since then, everywhere the British Army has gone so, too, has the Land Rover. As each new model has been introduced by the manufacturer so the Army has ordered it in large quanti-

The long wheelbase Land Rover chassis has, on occasions, been specially modified for military purposes. Shorland built this armoured car (left) for military customers, including the Ulster Defence Regiment, on a Series III one-ton chassis. The 'Pink Panther' Land Rover (below) is based on a 109-inch Land Rover and was built for the British Army's élite SAS regiment for use in desert operations where they were painted pink – hence the nickname. The regiment still uses similar vehicles called 'pinkies' which are based on One Ten high-capacity Land Rover pickups. They came to prominence in the Gulf War. Both the armoured car and the Pink Panther are preserved by The Dunsfold Land Rover Trust.

ties. It has used short and long wheebase variants with canvas tilts as well as more specialized models such as ambulance-bodied LWB models and models produced exclusively for them, including the 101 Forward Control and the Lightweight.

The 101 Forward Control was a large and imposing 4x4 built for the military after the demise of the civilian forward control models. It was V8-powered and differed considerably from most of the other Land Rover products then being made. The second of these was a Land Rover designed to be air-portable under helicopters. However, the payload of helicopters was not that great when the idea was mooted so Land Rover was asked to build a short wheelbase version that weighed less than the standard model. The result was the Lightweight which, as well as being lighter than a standard Series IIa, could be stripped down to lessen its weight further. The Lightweight is a flat-sided angular machine and remained in production through the Series III era, being phased out when helicopter payloads became so great that a lighter weight 4x4 was no longer necessary.

An interesting specialist conversion was the equipping of a number of 109-inch models for the British SAS. The conversions were carried out by Marshalls of Cambridge, England. This élite special forces unit served in places such as Oman during the Sixties and Seventies and required a more modern equivalent of the machine gun-equipped Jeeps of the Second World War. The result was the 'Pink Panther', although they were green when originally supplied to the army. The name Pink Panther originated from the shade of paint they were refinished in for operation in Oman. The name became shortened to Pinky and the current equivalents of the 109-inch patrol vehicle, based around Land Rover One Ten models, are still referred to as Pinkies.

Another impressive vehicle based around a Land Rover is the Shorland

Armoured car which was converted by Shorland, a Belfast, Northern Ireland-based company. A number of the vehicles were used in the province by the Ulster Defence Regiment during 'The Troubles'. Yet another conversion, intended for military use, was the half-track known as the Centaur and developed by Laird (Anglesey) Limited of Anglesey, Wales.

The Hummer

In military parlance, the Hummer is described as a HMMWV which stands for High Mobility Multi-purpose Wheeled Vehicle. It is manufactured by AM General but proved so popular that the manufacturers were forced to bring out a civilian version. This was introduced in 1993 and is powered by the same 6.2-litre diesel V8 that powers the military models. A three-speed automatic gearbox and coil sprung offset hub axles completes the package. The Hummer is an awesome off-roader and veteran desert racer Rod Hall competed in the Baja 1000 in one such vehicle.

The British Royal Air Force uses Land Rovers for a variety of duties, including this One Ten (top), for mountain rescue. This is a service that involves RAF personnel, experienced in searching for downed pilots through its search and rescue services, and who often cooperate with helicopter searches. The Auto-Union Munga (right) was built for the Bundeswehr, the postwar German Army. It is powered by a three-cylinder two-stroke engine and features permanent four-wheel-drive.

The Llama (above) was a prototype built by Land Rover for the British Army to replace its 101 Forward Control models. However, the vehicle was not chosen as a military vehicle so the project was cancelled and prototypes such as this were set to be scrapped. Luckily, this one was preserved by The Dunsfold Land Rover Trust. The Minerva (right) was a licence-built Land Rover built in Belgium for the Belgian Army in the early Fifties. The main difference between them and the British-built Land Rovers was the shape of the front wings.

CHAPTER SEVEN
COMPETITIVE FOUR-WHEEL-DRIVE

Motorsport forms an important part of four-wheel-drive activities around the world and ranges from huge International events to small competitions organized by local four-wheel-drive clubs. On each continent there are differing events but all have the same aim – that of competition between driver of four-wheel-drive vehicles. Some of the most spectacular events are the races; in North America there are a series of desert races run under the auspices of SCORE (Southern California Off Road Enterprises) and the HDRA (High Desert Racing Association), two of the most famous being the Mint 400 and the Baja 1000. The number suffix is an indication of the race's length in miles, while the name is relevant to its location. The Baja 1000 is run on the Baja peninsula in Mexico while the Mint 400 was based in Las Vegas, the Mint being a casino that was once a major sponsor. It is now, however, known as the Nissan 400, due to a change in sponsorship. The Baja 1000 has been running for more than 25 years and is renowned for its toughness, as is the Nissan 400.

Other American desert races include the Fireworks 250, the Las Vegas 250 and the Parker 400. There are fiercely contested classes for almost every type of pickup truck, 4x4 and off-road buggy. Some classes attract huge professional teams sponsored by 4x4 manufacturers and importers, for success in off-road racing results in increased showroom sales of 4x4s. In recent years both Ford,

Chevrolet and Toyota have made strong showings in the truck classes while Jeep Cherokee racers have gained honours in the Pro/Stock Mini-truck class. Other extensive sponsorship comes from parts and accessory manufacturers such as tyre companies, including BF Goodrich and Yokohama, who see off-road racing as an ideal testbed for their products. Manufacturers of shock absorbers and oil companies are also keen supporters of off-road racing.

A different sort of desert race, but one that is equally famous, is the Paris-Dakar. This long running 'raid' starts around Christmas every year and takes competitors from Paris through North Africa to Dakar on Africa's West Coast. There are classes for both stock and prototype 4x4s as well as other vehicles, including motorcycles. Many of the European and Japanese manufacturers have work's teams that regularly battle across miles of desert in pursuit of victory. Mitsubishi and Peugeot enter work's teams although there have been less expected entries in years past such as the V8-powered ARO driven by Frenchman Gérard Sarazin. The Rallye des Pharaohs is another competitive North African raid as is the Atlas Rally.

A major competitive event that involves 4x4s, but places little emphasis on speed, is the Camel Trophy. Billed as 1000 miles of adventure the annual event, which has been taking place for more than a decade, is unusual. It involves

Robby Gordon competing in the 1990 Presidente SCORE Baja 1000 desert race. The annual race was first run in 1963 and has evolved into a massive event supported by works' race teams. Gordon's Ford F-150 is supported by Ford and BF Goodrich among others. Although Gordon had won this event in 1989, he triple-rolled his truck in 1990 and was forced to retire.

teams from various countries – up to 18 different nationalities in recent years – driving identically-equipped 4x4s for approximately 1000 miles in a far-flung corner of the world. The aim of the event is for the convoy of both competitors' and event management vehicles to leave a start point and reach a destination over a three-week period. The competitive element is partially decided by a number of special tasks at both the beginning and end of the event and partially through teams voting for each other according to various criteria, one of them being Team Spirit. For every event since the first one when Jeep CJ7s were utilized, the Camel Trophy has used Land Rover products. For different years the Camel Trophy has used leaf sprung 109-inch Land Rovers, 90s and One Tens, when they were introduced, and Range Rovers. But for the last

few years it is Discovery models that have been used.

The Camel Trophy began when a small number of teams drove three Jeeps along a stretch of the Transamazonica Highway in South America – the legend was born and would continue every year. The second event was held in Sumatra in 1981 when a number of teams drove Range Rovers between Medan and Jambi. The event transferred to Papua, New Guinea when, again using Range Rovers, the teams drove between Mont Hagen and Madang. The event transferred to the African continent for 1983. In Zaire the teams drove Series III 88-inch wheelbase Land Rovers from Kinshasa to Kinsangani. It was back to South America and the Transamazonica Highway for 1984 where in Brazil the teams drove Land Rover 110 4x4s. In 1985, the event

moved to Borneo and, using Land Rover 90s, journeyed between Samarinda and Balikpapan. Another continent was visited for the first time in 1986 when the event covered the route between Cooktown and Darwin in northern Australia – again the teams drove Land Rover 90s. Diesel Range Rovers made their debut as Camel Trophy vehicles for the 1987 event when the destination was Madagascar. The route driven stretched from Diego Suarez to Fort Dauphin. In 1988 the Camel Trophy took Land Rover 110s to Sulawesi where they were driven from Manado to Ujang Padang by the competitors. It was back to the Amazon for 1989 when Land Rover 110s were driven from Alta Floresta to Manaus. The 1990 event took competitors deep into Siberia and to the shores of Lake Baikal and this year saw the Land Rover

The Camel Trophy is billed as '1000 miles of adventure', and, in 1991, the adventurers traversed Tanzania, from the east coast port of Dar Es Salaam in Tanzania to finish up in the tiny republic of Burundi, on Lake Tanganyika. Here (above), a Land Rover Discovery is arriving at a refuelling point.

Winning a place on a Camel Trophy team is an arduous process involving tasks, such as bridge building (right), where conditions are often very similar to those that will be encountered on the event itself.

During the 1991 event (above) the British Team of Tim Dray and Andrew Street are seen bringing their Land Rover Discovery across a river. The turbo diesel engine is protected by a roof height air intake positioned at the side of the windscreen to prevent water ingress.

Discovery TDi make its first appearance in the familiar Camel livery, the teams driving from Bratsk to Irkutsk.

In 1990, the Camel Trophy returned to Africa and for the first time visited two countries, Tanzania and Burundi. The teams drove TDi Discovery models from Dar Es Salaam on the East African Coast to Bujumbura on Lake Tanganyika. For 1993, the event progressed to Guyana where the teams once again used the Land Rover Discovery, as they have done up to the present time, and drove from Manaus to Georgetown. The event had a slightly dif-ferent emphasis in Sabah, Malaysia, in 1993 because the event negotiated a cir-cuitous route that commenced and finished in Kota Kinabalu. In 1994 the Camel Trophy visited three countries, Argentina, Paraguay and Chile. The route took the teams from the Iguazu Falls in Argentina to Hornitos in Chile. In 1995 the event was dubbed *Mundo Maya* and started in Lamanai, Belize, before proceeding through Mexico, Guatemala, El Salvador, Honduras to eventually finish in Xunantunich, also in Belize. The 1996 event took the teams from 20 countries to Kalimantan in Borneo where they drove east to west from Samarinda to Pontianak along the trail line of a suggested Trans-Borneo road.

Teams for the Camel Trophy from each country are usually selected from the thou-sands who apply each year through a series of practical tests that include physical fitness, mechanical aptitude and a degree of stamina as well as the right attitude. Each Camel Trophy brings its difficulties and hardships – impassable tracks which require considerable winching expertise and long days that mean sleep can be rare at times.

Ivan 'Ironman' Stewart driving his Toyota truck (above) in the annual Nissan 400. The truck has a number of sponsors including Yokohama tyres and is prepared by Precision Preparation Inc.

BF Goodrich have also supported off-road racers in the U.K. This buggy (above right) is based on Range Rover components and is raced under the auspices of the Northern Off-Road Club. The Chevrolet truck (right) American Thunder is raced in desert events by Scoop Vessels with support from BF Goodrich.

CHAPTER EIGHT
THE ENTHUSIAST SCENE

Worldwide, four-wheel-drive attracts any number of enthusiasts for as many reasons as there are makes of vehicle. Some join a club to meet like-minded people for recreational off-road driving – others join an owners' club as a way of keeping a rare or ageing 4x4 on the road through contact with other enthusiasts of the marque where they can expect mutual support through supply of spares and restoration information. Still more are interested in their 4x4s as an item of military history and go to enormous lengths to retain their vehicle's original specification: a less conservative bunch will spend their time building the most extrovert 4x4 machine imaginable or spend time modifying them for specific pursuits such as rock crawling and mud bogging. These two activities require entirely different approaches; rock crawling needs huge tyres and exceptionally low gear and differential ratios to enable the 4x4 to climb huge rocks and difficult rock-strewn paths, such as California's famous Rubicon trail to Lake Tahoe. A mud bogger will require a set of paddle-type tyres to provide traction in sloppy mud and, where it is timed against the clock, a performance engine.

There are those who use a relatively standard 4x4 to negotiate trails and tracks as a way of enjoying the outdoors or getting to favourite fishing spots. In some parts of the world a sport known as trialling is popular. This involves pairs of canes which mark out a number of sections over difficult ground which competing vehicles attempt to negotiate gaining penalty points for hitting canes or failing to complete the section. The rules vary between countries but the idea is the same and whoever has the least penalty points, when all the sections have been completed, wins. In Great Britain, these events are run by organizations such as the AWDC (All Wheel Drive Club) and Association of Rover Clubs constituent clubs.

Because Land Rovers are plentiful in Great Britain, their country of origin, there are numerous Land Rover Clubs. Some, such as The Series I Club, are designed for owners of a specific model while others are regional and more competitive in their outlook. There are also Land Rover clubs worldwide, including countries such as Zimbabwe, South Africa, Canada and the U.S.A. In America there are clubs in Virginia, Colorado,

This Daihatsu Fourtrak (left and far left) was prepared for an overland 'raid' from Paris, France to Peking, China by Deborah Turness who completed the journey with a number of other 4x4s.

(Above) The Austin Gipsy Club is an owners club dedicated to keeping these relatively rare 4x4s on the road.

Quite a different enthusiast-owned 4x4 is Ole Yeller (right) which was built by putting a Chevrolet pickup truck body on a 4x4 chassis and running gear.

Washington and California while in Canada Land Rover clubs can be found in Ontario and British Columbia. Jeep Clubs exist worldwide in places as far apart as Germany and Brazil and, of course, North America. There are clubs for much rarer 4x4s, too; a thriving British-based club helps enthusiasts keep their Austin Gipsy 4x4s running and in Indianapolis, U.S.A. the Scout and International Harvester Light Truck Association can be found. Jeepers' Jamborees, off-road gatherings for American Jeep owners, exist all over the United States and one takes place annually in France, too.

Simply put, the enthusiasm for four-wheel-drive vehicles worldwide is rampant; a common t-shirt slogan reads, 'Four wheel drive owners do it in the dirt'. There are specialist garages around the world who restore, repair and modify four-wheel-drive vehicles to suit their owners' tastes. There are even specialists who will fabricate complete vehicles, either in the form of heavily modified early Jeeps or Land Rovers in the way of street-rod builders but for off-road use or there are those who build small numbers of complete 4x4 vehicles to their own design. With four-wheel-drive almost anything is possible.

The Haggis Hunter *(left) is a modified Toyota HiLux pickup truck. Its name, and the flag flying above the cab, identify it as a Scottish truck.*

A much more basic but equally well built 4x4 is this early Land Rover (bottom left). Hidden under its almost standard bodywork are the axles, chassis, engine and gearbox of a Range Rover. The shortened wheelbase and coil springs make it an effective off-road machine.

Cruising the beach (bottom centre) is a popular pastime on a sunny day, as these red Jeeps – a Wrangler YJ and a Mahindra CJ – demonstrate.

Another enthusiast-owned Wrangler (bottom right) is this one belonging to Ron Martin of Sheffield, England.

*Clockwise from bottom left; a Jeep
Wrangler on Daytona beach, Florida; a
Toyota Land Cruiser with roof tent in
Glencoe, Scotland; a modified Jeep CJ7 on
Daytona Beach; and a Sixties International
Scout preserved by John Marchant.*